Reminiscing
a Whimsicals Collection

By Terri Degenkolb

Reminiscing
a Whimsicals Collection

By Terri Degenkolb
Edited by Judy Pearlstein
Tech edited by Nan Doljac
Design by Brian Grubb
Quilt Photographs by Aaron Leimkuehler
Illustrations by Terri Degenkolb
Production Assistance by Jo Ann Groves

Published by Kansas City Star Books
1729 Grand Boulevard
Kansas City, Missouri 64108

First edition, first printing
ISBN: 978-1-933466-80-4

Printed in the United States of America
By Walsworth Publishing Co.
Marceline, Missouri

To order copies, call StarInfo, 816-234-4636
(Say "Operator.")

KANSAS CITY STAR BOOKS
Kansas City, Missouri

KANSAS CITY STAR QUILTS
Continuing the Tradition

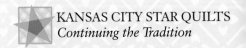

PickleDish.com
The Quilter's Home Page

www.Pickledish.com http://www.pickledish.com/

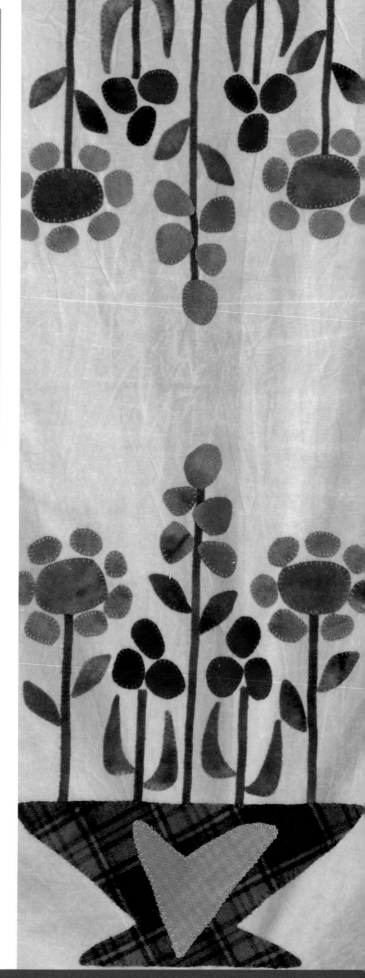

Acknowledgements

Thank You, Thank, You!

...to all of you who have purchased my books, patterns, and fabrics over the years. Your notes and feedback are greatly appreciated.

...to Doug Weaver and Diane McLendon at *The Kansas City Star* for suggesting this project and giving me this opportunity.

....to my Mom and Dad. I never would have started on this journey if not for your support, encouragement, and your continuing belief in me and my dreams.

...to my kids, Scott and Tyler, for putting up with my inability to set work aside to get dinner on the table, my constant reminders to turn the music down because "I need to work," and for reminding me why I need to slow down.

...to my husband, Tom, for his contant understanding, help, and love. I couldn't do any of this without him by my side.

Table of contents

Acknowledgements 3

The Author 5

Introduction 6

General Notes and Construction 7

The Projects 10-93

Other Star Books 94

projects

1 Garden Stroll at Midnight
10-15

2 Rusted Moons
16-23

3 Angel in My Garden
24-31

4 Pathways
32-37

5 Whimsical Threads
38-43

6 Crazy Strips
44-51

7 Not Quite Christmas
52-57

8 Spring Flowers
58-61

9 Pineapple Penny Rug
62-67

10 Night Blooms Pillow
68-71

11 Wildflowers
72-77

12 Old Buttons Pillow
78-83

13 Peeking Tom
84-87

14 Tag Along Tote
88-94

A Few Words About Me

Terri grew up in rural Indiana, surrounded by corn fields, animals, and parents who always encouraged her to use her imagination. After several years in the working world, where there was little time for creativity, she quit her job to stay at home with her two boys and was once again encouraged by her parents, along with her husband, to use her desire to create. And Whimsicals was born. Ten years later, with numerous self-published books and patterns, along with several fabric lines completed, she still loves coming up with new things. Because of her fascination with color, textures, and the "old crafts," her projects take on many forms - from quilts and penny rugs to embroidery and jewelry - and are a mix of primitive and folk art, with a healthy dose of tradition thrown in. Still living in Indiana, she loves the variety and freedom that comes with her work and gets inspiration from roaming through the antique shops and enjoying the nature surrounding her. Although working at home has its own challenges, she feels blessed to have the opportunity to share time with her kids and still do what she loves to do - create. To see more, visit her web site at whimsicalquilts.com

Introduction

Life takes us in many directions and along differing paths. I love the thought that our lives are not made up of days, weeks, or even years, but of the moments that we experience through each one. Those moments shape who we are and who we become.

And so it is when we make a quilt. Every piece we add is like one of those moments. The fabrics we choose, the decisions we make, what we are feeling at the time, all work their way into each quilt and determine what it will become. That is what makes each quilt our own.

Each of these projects, whether made several years ago or just last week, has a portion of me in it. Maybe it was a memory from childhood that helped shape it, or a specific hope that inspired me to make it. Maybe when you see one, it will take you back in time, or spark a new idea.

So sit down with me. Do a little reminiscing. **Let your mind wander and enjoy!**

General Notes

Seams and Measurements

Use 1/4" seams unless noted otherwise. Measurements given include the seam allowance.

For some pieces, we have given measurements of pieces that will need to be trimmed after piecing. We would much rather stitch and trim than cut to the exact size and find that our finished blocks are too small because of a difference in seam size. Unfortunately, at times our stitching isn't perfect (imagine that!) and we really don't like to do "reverse sewing!"

None of the appliqué pieces have seam allowance added. Take this into account when preparing your pieces for applique. If you are using a traditional appliqué technique where the edges will be turned under, make sure you add the 1/4" needed for the seam allowance!

Binding

All binding yardages are based on double thickness binding cut 2 1/4" wide on the straight grain of the fabric.

However, with that being said, my preference is to cut 2 1/8" strips on the bias. I find the double thickness with the folded edge already on the back, along with the added stretch of the bias, makes the binding easier to stitch down. It also helps the finished quilt and the corners lie nice and flat.

The yardage given will accommodate either cutting method.

Making Freezer Paper Templates

Trace the design onto the matte side of freezer paper, then cut this out along the drawn lines.

To use the template for cutting fabrics, place the freezer paper on the fabric with the shiny side down (against the fabric) and press it in place with a warm dry iron. This temporarily adheres it to the fabric, giving you a nice solid piece to cut around without anything shifting. Cut the fabric as indicated for each method. These can be used several times.

Note that the seam allowance is included in each template used for piecing. No seam allowance has been added for appliqué templates.

Fabrics

We use 100% cotton fabric and 100% wool. If you are going to spend hours on a project, it's worth the extra money to get quality fabrics that will last.

The look of the hand-dyed wool is great, but if it is not available in your area, you can felt your own wool by washing it in warm water in the washing machine with a cold water rinse, then drying it in the dryer. This shrinks the wool fibers, tightening them to allow you to appliqué without fusible webbing or turning the edges under.

Cutting and Piecing from Templates

Trace each piece onto freezer paper as described above. As you trace the templates, make sure that you mark each one with its corresponding letter to keep them straight. Also mark the grainline on the pieces indicated as it is important to keep these going with the grain to avoid bias edges on the outside of the block (very unstable!)

After cutting the pieces, lay them close to your machine in the proper positions before peeling off the freezer paper. This makes piecing much easier on the brain!

Freezer Paper Appliqué

There are countless techniques for cotton appliqué, but this is my preferred method.

First, make a template from freezer paper as described above.

Iron the template to the wrong side of the fabric. Cut the fabric out around the template a scant 1/4" from the edge. Clip any curves and corners if necessary. There is no need to turn under edges that will be overlapped by another piece, but the 1/4" allowance still needs to be added.

With large, simple pieces, a quick way to prepare the piece is to spray the right side of the fabric lightly with spray starch. Turn it over and begin carefully pressing the edge under (using the freezer paper as the edge). When you are done, turn it back over (so the right side is up) and press it again. If you have trouble spots, spray some starch into a small container and "paint" it onto the seam allowance with a small paint brush. Now, you can remove the freezer paper and position the appliqué on your foundation.

NOTE

THE APPLIQUÉ TEMPLATES HAVE BEEN REVERSED for easy tracing when using the freezer paper applliqué method.

For small pieces, I sometimes find it faster and less frustrating to just get out my needle and thread. Again, using the edge of the freezer paper, turn the edge under as you baste through both layers of fabric and the freezer paper. Once done basting, you can lightly spray the right side with starch, press it, then remove the basting and freezer paper.

After preparing my appliqué, I use a long basting stitch and hand baste the pieces in place. This gives me enough control over the piece to position it as I baste it down, and makes it easily mobile, with no pins to come out or stick a finger unexpectedly.

At this point, you can choose to stitch the piece down by hand or machine. If you like hand work, stitch the pieces in place with a small blind stitch with matching thread. If your sewing machine has a nice blind stitch or blanket stitch, use matching thread to stitch everything in place.

Primitive Wool Appliqué

Make a template from freezer paper as described above.

Place the freezer paper template on the wool with the shiny side against the wool. Cut the piece out (no need to add 1/4" seam), then carefully peel the freezer paper off the wool.

I sometimes apply fusible web to the back of my wool, especially when sharp points are involved, to keep the wool from raveling while I stitch it down. With the larger pieces, I cut away the center portion of the fusible web (about 1/8" - 1/4" inside the cutting line) to keep the piece softer and more pliable. Many times, I don't actually fuse the piece to the foundation, as it is hard to get it to stick for long without "mashing" the wool fibers, but it gives it enough stability to make stitching easier.

After positioning the appliqué pieces on the foundation and basting them in place, stitch them down with 2 or 3 strands of embroidery floss. Different stitches can be used to secure these in place, as each has its own look. A simple running stitch just inside the edge gives a very simple look to the finished piece. A whipstitch is a bit more primitive looking, while the buttonhole stitch is the traditional way of finishing off these pieces. Experiment with them and choose the one you like best!

Making Bias Strips for Stems

Bias strips are great for making gracefully curved stems and vines. To make them, cut strips on the bias (at a 45 degree angle from the straight grain of the fabric). These can be cut to make any width you like. When we have used them, we have given the width we cut the strips in the instructions. The general rule is to cut them three times the desired finished width. You can make long strips by piecing them together with a bias seam. Just make sure you press your seams open to reduce bulk.

Fold the strips into thirds, WRONG sides together, and machine baste down the center. When you stitch the bias strip to your foundation, place the side with the raw edge against the foundation and stitch along each edge with small blind stitches. Remove the basting after you finish stitching it in place.

Garden stroll at Midnight

We originally made this quilt in a light version and a dark version. One ended up at my house, the other at mom's. I love the dark one, which hangs over my bed. To me, it looks like the flowers are just having a bit of fun, dancing in the night!

**Quilt by
Terri Degenkolb**

**Quilted by
Marilyn Harding**

48" x 48"

What's Needed

- ☐ Nine black backgrounds: 9" x 11" pieces
- ☐ Nine accent fabrics: 9" x 9" pieces
- ☐ Fat quarter of dark brown for center squares
- ☐ 2/3 yard medium brown
- ☐ 1 1/4 yards black for border
- ☐ Fat quarter felted green wool for stems/leaves
- ☐ Twelve 7" squares felted wool for flowers
- ☐ 3 yards for backing
- ☐ 1/2 yard for binding

Garden Stroll

Cutting the Pieces

- From each of the **nine black background fabrics**, cut:
  4 — 2 1/2" squares for a total of 36 squares (A).
  5 — 2 7/8" squares for a total of 45 squares (half-square triangle B).

- From each of the **nine accent fabrics**, cut:
  3 — 2 7/8" squares for a total of 27 squares (half-square triangle B).
  1 — 4 7/8" squares for a total of 9 squares (C).

- From the **dark brown fabric**, cut four 81/2" squares.

- From the **medium brown fabric**, cut the following:
  4 — 8 7/8" squares
  2 — 9 1/4" squares - cut twice diagonally (D)
  2 — 5 1/4" squares - cut twice diagonally (F)
  4 — 2 1/4" squares - cut once diagonally (G)
  4 — 2 7/8" squares (half square triangle H)

- From the **black border fabric**, cut the following:
  4 — 8 1/2" squares
  4 — 8 7/8" squares
  4 — 4 1/2" x 24 1/2" strips
  8 — 2 1/2" squares
  4 — 4 7/8" squares - cut once diagonally (E)
  4 — 2 1/4" squares - cut once diagonally (G)
  8 — 2 7/8" squares (half square triangle H)

Making the Blocks
(9 blocks finishing to 8")

Pair each black background with an accent fabric and make 9 blocks as follows:

Cut the 2 7/8" squares (B) once diagonally. With the resulting triangles, stitch together six half square units. Square these up to 2 1/2".

With 4 of the half square units and the 2 1/2" black background squares (A), stitch together two larger units as shown in Diagram 1. Square these up to 4 1/2".

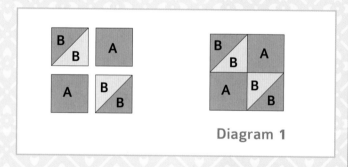

Diagram 1

Cut the 47/8" accent fabric square (C) once diagonally. With the resulting triangles, the remaining black background triangles, and the remaining half square units, stitch together two units as shown in Diagram 2. Square these up to 4 1/2".

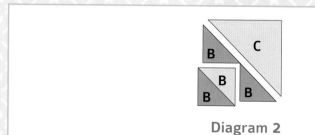

Diagram 2

Assemble the block as shown in Diagram 3. Square these nine blocks up to 8 1/2".

Cut the medium brown and black 4 7/8" squares once diagonally. With the resulting triangles, make eight half square units. Square these up to 8 1/2".

Making the Corner Units & Border

With the (D) and (E) triangles, stitch together eight border end units as shown in Diagram 4. Note that 4 of these are mirror images!

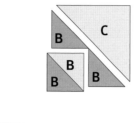

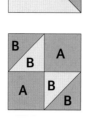

Diagram 3

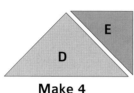

Make 4   **Make 4**

Diagram 4

Stitch these to the ends of the 24 1/2" border strips. (See the Overall Piecing Diagram.)

Cut the 2 7/8" medium brown and black border squares (H) once diagonally. With the resulting triangles, stitch together eight half square units. Square these up to 2 1/2".

Referring to Diagram 5, make four corner units as follows:

- Make 4 four patch units with the the half squares (H) and the 2 1/2" black border squares.

- Stitch the remaining eight black border triangles (H) to the medium brown triangles (F).

- Stitch together eight G/G units with the medium brown and black (G) triangles.

- Stitch the units together as shown.

Make 4

Diagram 5

Finishing

Referring to the Overall Piecing Diagram, stitch the center section of the quilt together. Add the border pieces and the corner units.

Prepare the applique pieces using your favorite method and stitch them to the quilt using the photo as a guide for placement. Felted wool was used on the quilt shown, and was stitched down with 2 strands of embroidery floss.

Layer the quilt with batting and a backing, quilt and bind.

Piecing Diagram

Bias Strips for Stems

To make cotton bias strips for stems, cut strips on the bias (at a 45 degree angle from the straight grain of the fabric) three times the desired finished width. To make a long strip, piece several strips together with bias seams, pressing the seams open.

Fold the strips into thirds, WRONG sides together, and machine baste down the center. When you stitch the bias strip to your foundation, place the side with the raw edge against the foundation and stitch along each edge with small blind stitches. Remove the basting after you finish stitching it in place.

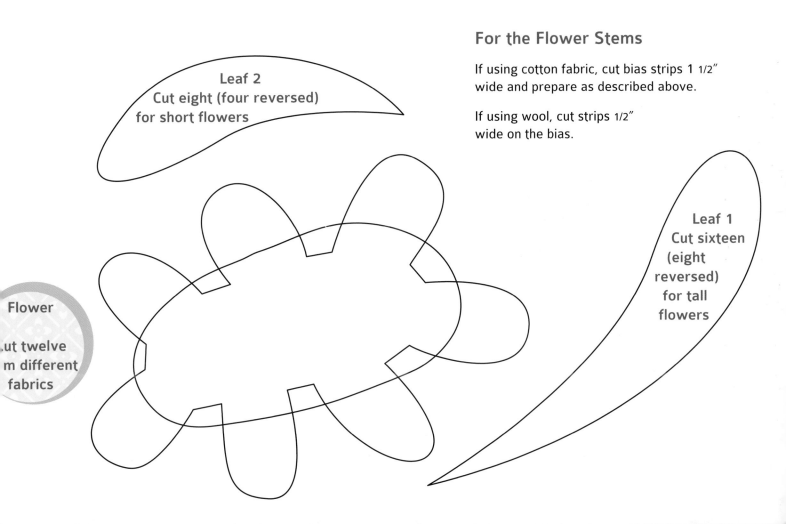

For the Flower Stems

If using cotton fabric, cut bias strips 1 1/2" wide and prepare as described above.

If using wool, cut strips 1/2" wide on the bias.

Leaf 2
Cut eight (four reversed) for short flowers

Flower
Cut twelve from different fabrics

Leaf 1
Cut sixteen (eight reversed) for tall flowers

Rusted moons

Fall in Indiana is my favorite season.

To see the leaves change colors is amazing. By using rust colors for all the moons, then adding the other colors of the fall, I feel like I can enjoy the season just a little longer inside, where it's warm and dry.

Made by Terri Degenkolb
Quilted by Tracie Bunce

Finished Size: 40" x 52"

What's Needed

- Fat 1/8 of six light fabrics
- Total of 1/2 yard dark fabrics
- 1/2 yard for sashing
- 1/4 yard for first border
- 1/4 yard for second border
- 1/2 yard for third border
- Scraps for appliqué
- 3 yards for backing
- 1/2 yard for binding

Cutting the Pieces

- From the **six light fabrics**, cut:

  a total of 6 — 9 1/2" x 9 1/2" squares for backgrounds (A).

  a total of 10 — 2 1/2" x 9 1/2" strips for borders (B).

  a total of 4 — 2 1/2" squares for the corners (C).

- From the **various dark fabrics**, cut:

  a total of 48 — 2" squares (D).

  a total of 48 — 2 1/2" squares (E).

- From the sashing fabric, cut:

  17 — 3 1/2" x 9 1/2" strips (F).

  14 — 2 1/2" x 3 1/2" strips (G).

From the first border fabric, cut four strips 1 3/4" x width of fabric. Stitch these together to make one long strip, then cut two strips 43 1/2" long for the side borders and two strips 34" long for the top and bottom borders.

From the second border fabric, cut 5 strips 1 1/4" x width of fabric. Stitch these together to make one long strip, then cut two strips 46" long for the side borders and two strips 35 1/2 " long for the top/ bottom borders.

Rusted moons

From the third border fabric, cut five strips 3" x width of fabric. Stitch these together to make one long strip, then cut two side borders 47 1/2" long and two top/bottom borders 40 1/2" long.

From the various scraps, prepare the appliqué pieces.

Note that you will need six moons, a few of which are reversed.

Making the Blocks

(six blocks finishing to 9")
Draw a diagonal line on the wrong side of the dark 2 1/2" (E) squares.

On the six background squares (A), stitch 2 1/2" squares on the corners as follows: With right sides together, place the square on the corner and stitch along the drawn diagonal line. Press the seam toward the small square and trim off the excess 1/4" from the stitching line as shown in Diagram 1. Square these up to 9 1/2". Appliqué.
Note: I did not put a face on my cat. Embroider if desired.

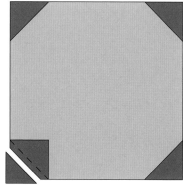

Diagram 1

Repeat this with the 10 (B) border strips (Diagram 2). Square these up to 2 1/2" x 9 1/2".

Diagram 2

Using the four remaining 2 1/2" (E) squares and the four (C) squares, make four half-square blocks as follows: Place a light and dark square right sides together. Stitch along the drawn line of the (E) square, press the seam toward the dark square, then trim off the excess 1/4" from the stitching line. Square these up to 2 1/2".
Note: This method was used to keep cutting consistent and to make the four corners scrappy.

Diagram 3

With the 48 dark 2" squares (D), make twelve four patch blocks as shown in Diagram 4. Square these up to 3 1/2".

Diagram 4

Putting it Together

Position the appliqué pieces on the six foundation squares and stitch in place. Following the Piecing Diagram, stitch together the sashing and blocks.

Add the borders by first stitching on the two side pieces, then adding the top and bottom.

Layer with batting and backing, quilt and bind!

Piecing Diagram

Designs have been reversed for fusible web or freezer paper applique methods.

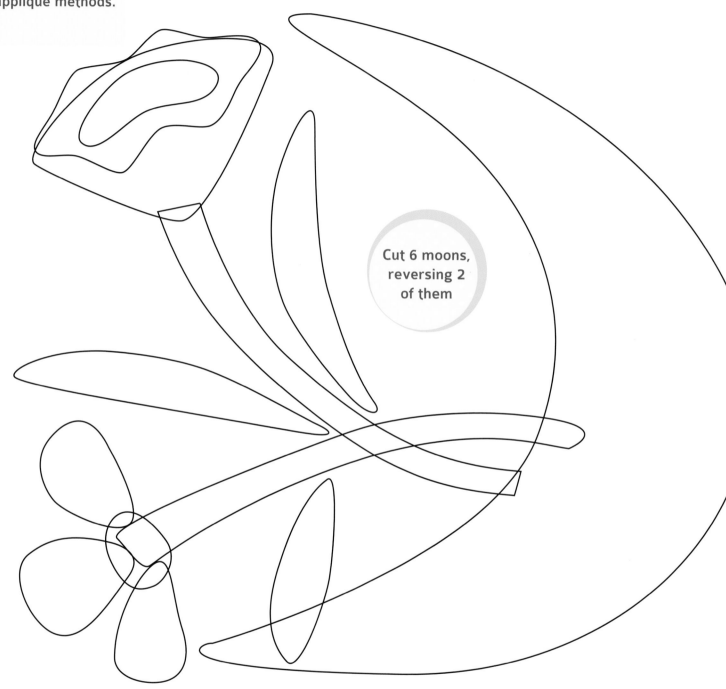

Cut 6 moons, reversing 2 of them

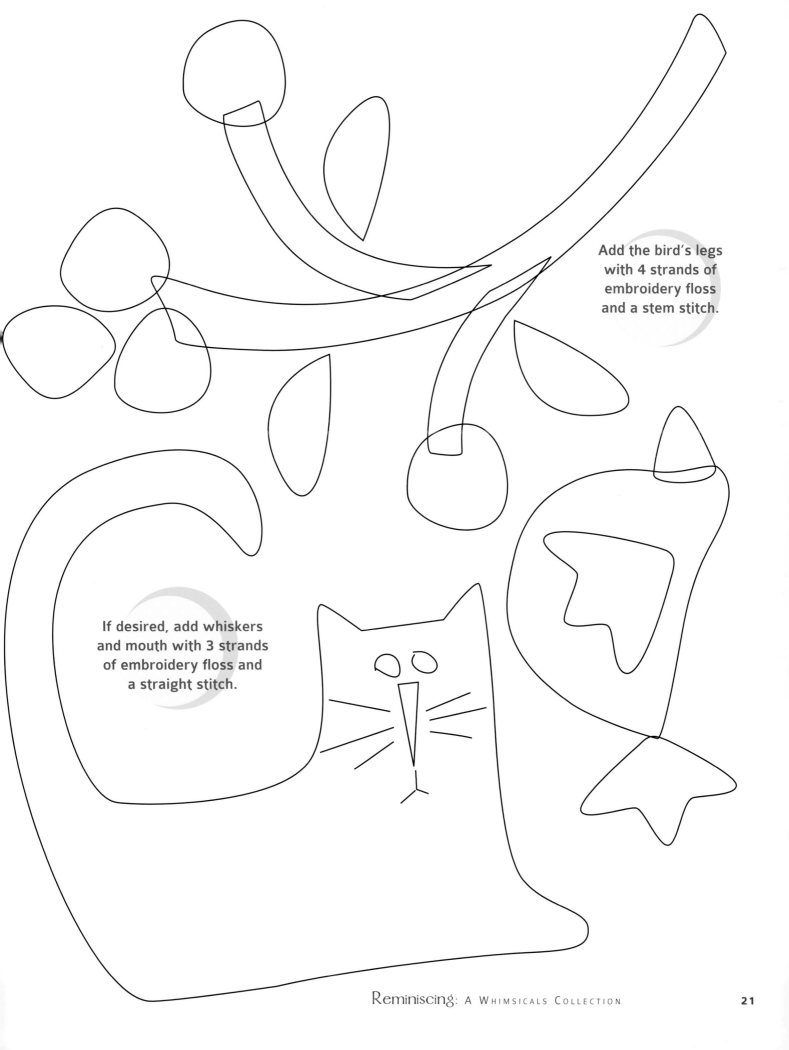

Add the bird's legs
with 4 strands of
embroidery floss
and a stem stitch.

If desired, add whiskers
and mouth with 3 strands
of embroidery floss and
a straight stitch.

Angel in my garden

I think we all have guardian angels that watch over us and guide us. Some days, I feel them in the warning honk of a car horn, telling me to watch out, while other days it may be in the whisper of the leaves, reminding me to slow down and enjoy the beauty of God's creation.

This angel hangs in my sewing room. She is my reminder that everything I love - from my family all the way down to the blades of grass in my yard - is being protected by someone far greater than me.

Made by Terri Degenkolb

Finished Size: 25" x 29"

What's Needed

- ☐ Fat 1/4 for background
- ☐ 1/4 yard dark fabric for inner border
- ☐ 1/4 yard light fabric for middle border
- ☐ 1/4 yard dark fabric for outer border
- ☐ 1/4 yard for binding
- ☐ 3/4 yard for backing

Felted wool as follows:

- ☐ 9" x 17" plaid for angel body
- ☐ 7" x 12" gold for flower
- ☐ 6" x 11" brown for flower
- ☐ 5" x 7" green for stems and leaf
- ☐ 7" x 7" gold for wing
- ☐ 4" x 6" dark gold for horn
- ☐ 2" x 7" red for dress trim
- ☐ 2" x 5" brown for hair
- ☐ 5" x 6" tan for hands, head, legs
- ☐ 2" x 3" light gold for flower dots
- ☐ Embroidery floss to match

Cutting the Pieces

- ☐ From the background fabric, cut a piece 16 1/2" x 20 1/2".
- ☐ From inner border fabric, cut six 3 1/2" squares, two strips 1 1/2" x 16 1/2", and two strips 1 1/2" x 22 1/2".
- ☐ From the middle border fabric cut twelve 3 1/2" squares and twenty-two 2 1/2" squares.
- ☐ From the outer border fabric, cut six 3 1/2" squares, two strips 2" x 22 1/2", and two strips 2" x 29 1/2".

Angel in my garden

Assembly

Make freezer paper templates for the applique pieces and cut them from the felted wool indicated. Note that the lines on the wing are cut out and discarded. Position these on the foundation and stitch in place with 3 strands of embroidery floss and a whip stitch.

Note that the method used to make the quarter squares will make two complete blocks from each set of half squares. You will end up with twelve squares, one of which will not be used.

Using the 3 1/2" squares, make half squares as follows:

Layer six of the middle border squares (A) with the inner border squares (C). Layer the remaining six middle border squares (A) with the outer border squares (B).

Cut along the diagonal of each set and stitch the resulting triangles together along the diagonal. (See Diagram 1)

Press the seam toward the B and C fabrics. (Diagram 2)

With right sides together and lights against darks, layer the A/B half squares with the A/C half squares, nesting the seams.

Cut along the diagonal perpendicular to the seam. Stitch the resulting triangle units together along the diagonal.

You will have twelve quarter square blocks as shown in Diagram 3.

Discard one of these and square the remaining eleven units up to measure 2 1/2".

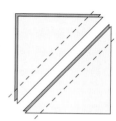

Diagram 1

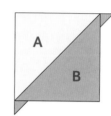
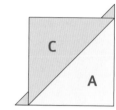

Diagram 2

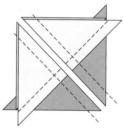
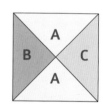

Diagram 3

Piecing Diagram

Stitch the two 16 1/2" inner border strips to the sides of the foundation. Add the remaining two inner border strips to the top and bottom.

Referring to the Piecing Diagram, use the 2 1/2" middle border squares and the quarter squares made above to piece together the side borders and the top/bottom borders. Add these to the foundation.

Add the two 22 1/2" outer border strips to the sides and then the remaining outer border strips to the top and bottom.

Add backing and batting, then quilt and bind!

Angel Wing

Cut out and discard shaded areas for foundation to show thru.

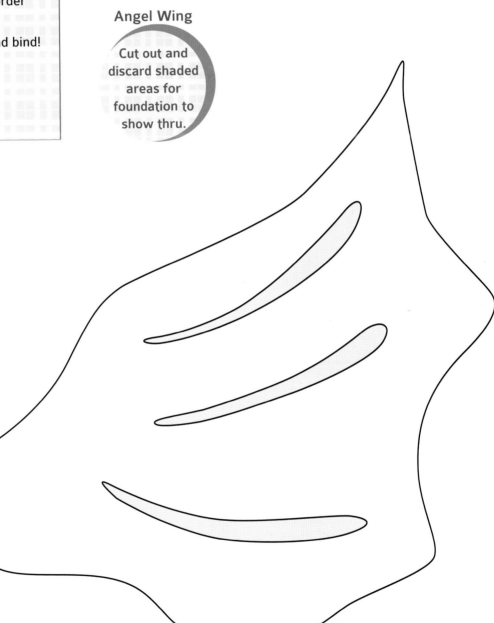

Angel
in my garden

Join here

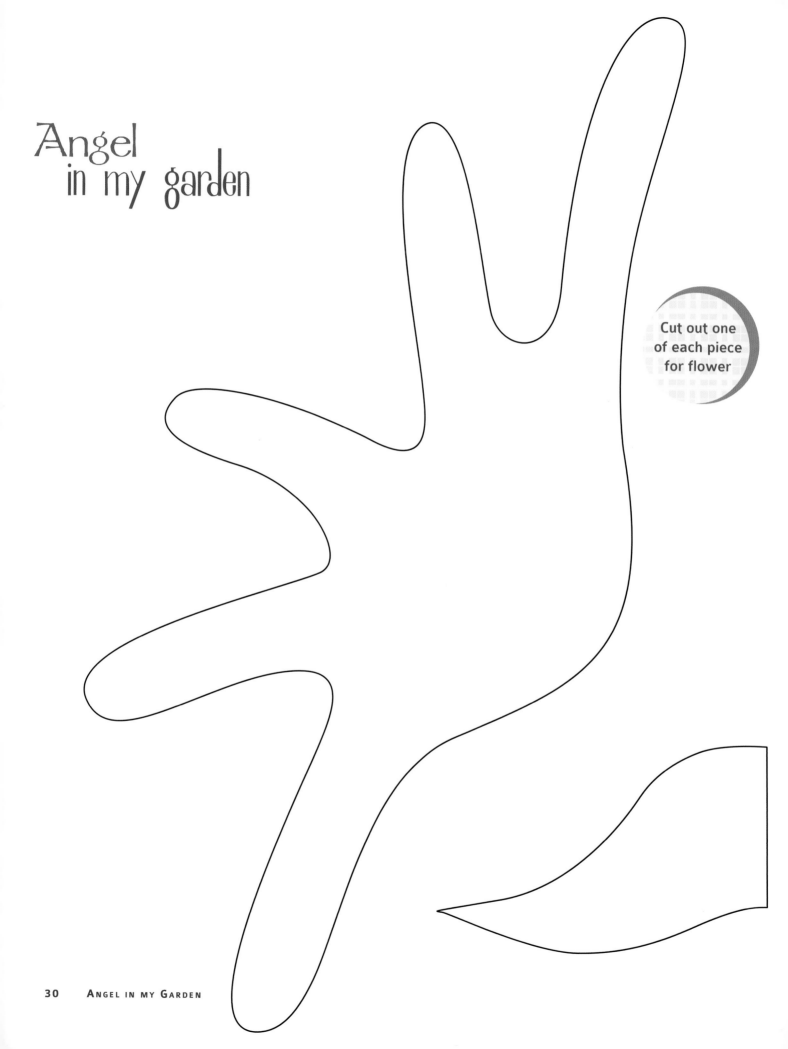

Angel
in my garden

Cut out one of each piece for flower

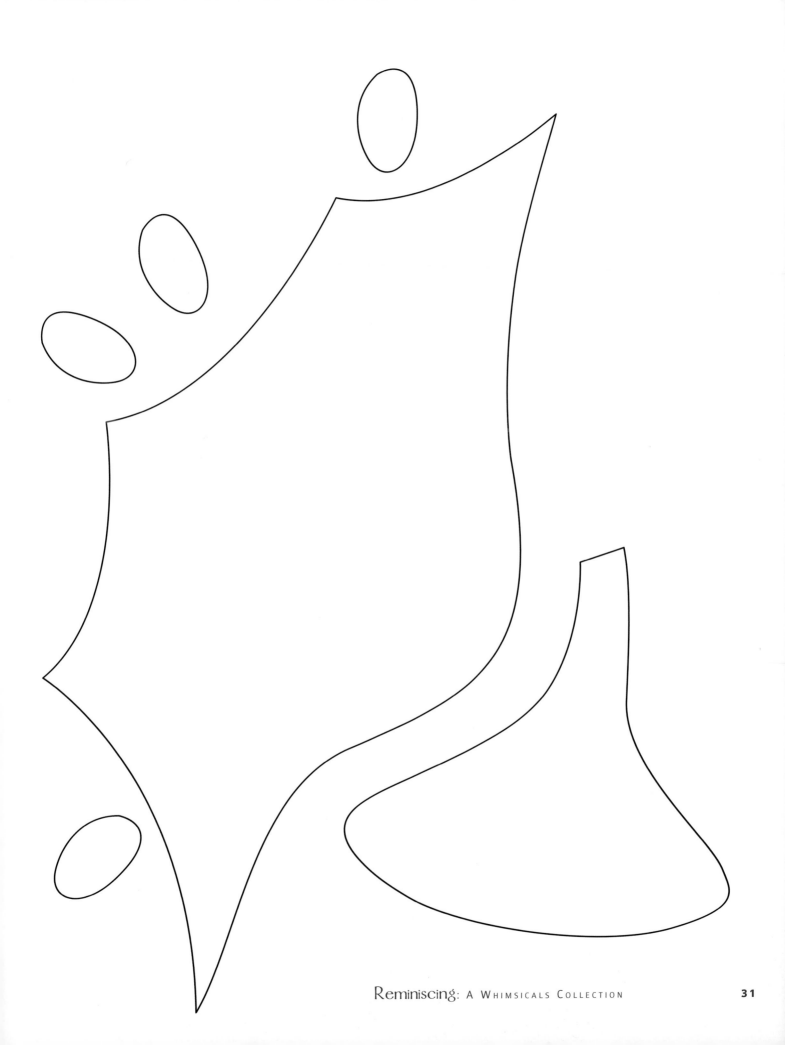

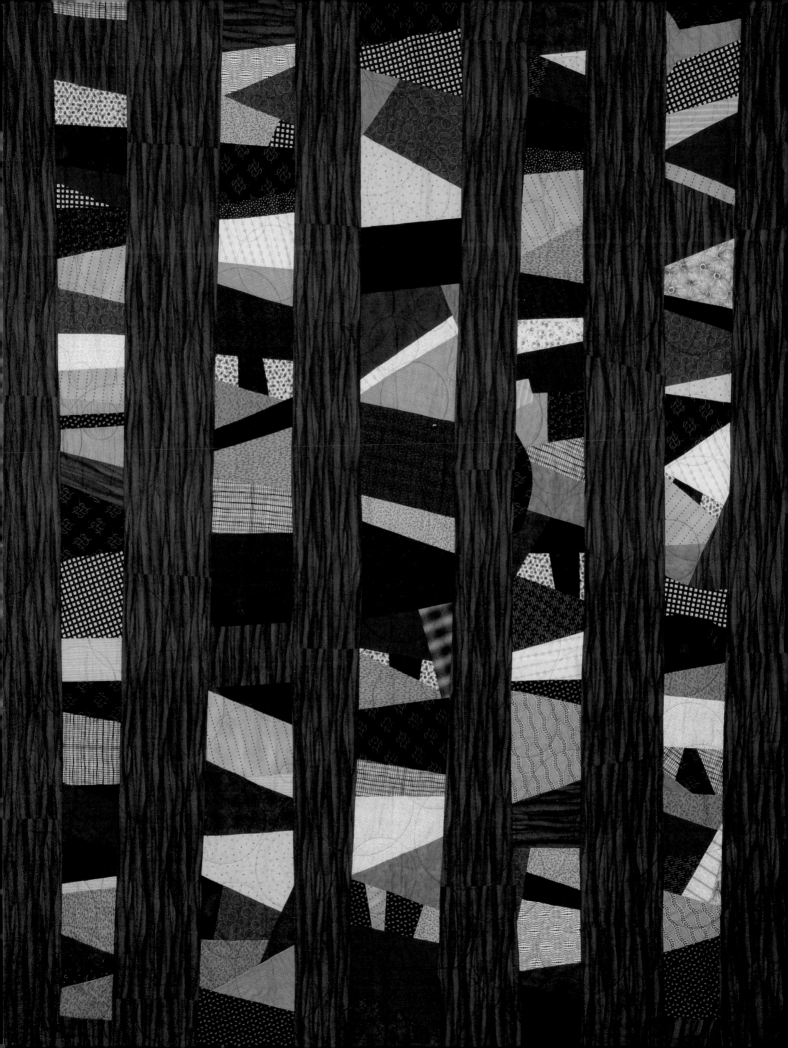

Pathways

My oldest son just graduated from high school.

Of course, I wanted to make him a quilt for the occasion. One that would remind him that there will always be a place for him to come "home" to, no matter where the journeys of his life take him. But it also needed to reflect his personality and tastes, which are much different from mine.

Being a creative individual himself, he knew what he wanted, or more what he DIDN'T want. No small pieces or intricate design - just big "random chunks of fabric" (those were his words) - and no appliqué.

With that in mind, I had the idea to make a strip quilt with wide bands of a single fabric separated by pieced strips. As I began cutting and stitching random pieces of fabrics together, this quilt kind of took on a life of its' own that just grew and evolved as I went. The result was a quilt that is very random, just like my son, and was a blast for me to make because it stripped away all the rules.

So, as he heads down another road in his life, one that will take him away from home, I pray that no matter where his life leads him, he will always be able to find the path back home, and tread along it often.

Terms

For the purpose of these instructions, strip refers to the vertical pieces of fabric and piece refers to the smaller horizontal fabrics that make up the pieced strips.

Warning

There are no definitive measurements for making this quilt. You must let yourself be free to make mistakes and wing it as you go! A good example: as I was trimming one of my pieced strips, I noticed a piece that was too short that would result in a hole along the seam. What did I do? I appliqued a piece over it, making the applique large enough to extend out into the seam, and voila! The hole was gone. Or, when a piece didn't seem like it would be big enough, I stitched several together before adding them to the strip.

Stitched by Terri Degenkolb
Quilted by Kathy Dye

Finished size of quilt shown: 88" x 107"

Most importantly, don't stress over a little wasted fabric and let yourself have fun.

General Instructions
Determine the Size

Determining the approximate finished size of the quilt will help you determine what size to shoot for when piecing the strips together. Think about proportion. Do you want the strips to be of equal width or do you want the solid strips wider than the pieced strips? Do you want a certain width strip along the sides to hang down on the side of your bed?

Pathways

General Instructions Determine the Size (cont)

To help get an idea, refer to the Possible Sizes and Proportioning Diagrams. Note that these are only ideas and estimates to get you thinking. If it helps, sketch your ideas and measurements on a piece of graph paper and keep it handy.

Cut the Solid Strips

These can be equal widths or varied. Cut the strips an inch or two wider than the desired finished width. This will give plenty of "play" when trimming and adding the pieced strips.

Depending on your fabric, you can choose to cut these either along the length of your fabric so that the strips are seamless, or you can cut your fabric crosswise and piece together enough for the length of your quilt.

When placing the seams in these strips, try to vary the placement on them so that your seams don't all end up running across the quilt at the same place. Also, consider stitching them together with a diagonal seam instead of a seam going straight across.

Make the Pieced Strips

These strips are randomly pieced. In many cases, I even ignored the grain of the fabric, just so I could have a stripe running at an odd angle.

Again, aim for piecing a strip a few inches wider than the finished width. Because of the way these are pieced together, it is unlikely that the strip will be perfectly straight, even with careful piecing.

Begin with two pieces of fabric each about 7" long. Add random pieces using any of the following methods, pressing the seams open where possible.

To add a piece at an angle without a straight edge:

Place both fabrics right side up, one on top of the other, with both facing the same way and the fabric to be added on the top. Cut at an angle as shown in Diagram 1.

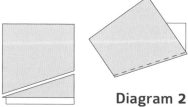

Diagram 1

Diagram 2

Diagram 3

With right sides together, stitch the seam as shown in Diagram 2.

Press the seam open. You should have a unit that looks something like Diagram 3.

To add a piece at an angle with a straight edge:
With right sides together, place the piece with a straight edge on top of the piece to be trimmed. Trim the excess even with the straight edge, then stitch the seam as shown in Diagram 4.

If the added piece isn't big enough, add a smaller piece as shown in Diagrams 5 and 6.

Continue adding pieces until the pieced strip is several inches longer than the desired length.

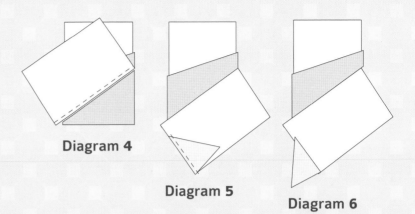

Diagram 4

Diagram 5

Diagram 6

Trim the Strips

Even if you very carefully stitch the pieces together for the pieced strips, chances are you will still end up with uneven edges, or maybe even a strip with a nice curve to it, like I did. There are two different ways to trim the strips - to be straight and equal in width from top to bottom, or to be curved and random.

Decide which method you like best, then trim all your pieced and solid strips to the desired widths. Refer to the Possible Sizes and Proportioning diagrams for ideas, or draw your plan out on graph paper. Remember that the idea is to have a quilt that is completely and uniquely yours!

Straight & Equal

It is by far easier to cut both the pieced strips and the alternating solid strips to be an equal width top to bottom. This is done with a rotary cutter and long ruler.

To determine what width to cut a pieced strip, be sure to take into account the uneven edges or be prepared to add an applique piece to cover up any holes.

Fold the strips into double or even triple thickness and cut them in the same way you would cut strips from a width of fabric, as shown in Diagram 7.

Stitch the strips together along the long edge.

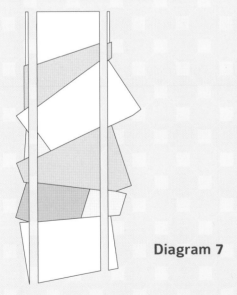

Diagram 7

Pathways

Curved and Random

The strips in the pictured quilt were cut randomly in width with no rulers.

To do this, you need a flat surface large enough to lay the two strips to be stitched together side by side for their entire length, and enough cutting mats underneath to stretch the entire length.

Lay a solid strip and a pieced strip side by side, ovelapping the pieced strip onto the solid one enough to trim a little off of both strips, as shown in Diagram 8. Draw your cutting line with chalk.

Trim the strips to be even in length. Then, cut through all the layers along your chalked line. Discard the excess fabric cut off. The two pieces should now match up as shown in Diagram 9.

With right sides together, pin the two strips together, matching the edges and easing in where necessary, then stitch them together.

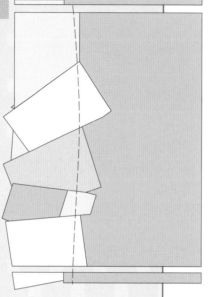

Diagram 8

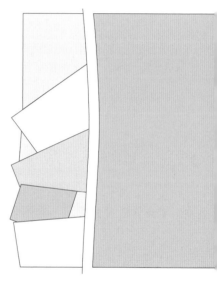

Diagram 9

Lap

Approx. Size: 53" x 70"

3 yards of main fabric

Total of 2 yards assorted fabrics

4 yards for backing

2/3 yard for binding

| 10" | 6" | 8" | 5" | 8" | 6" | 10" |

Twin
Approx. Size: 65" x 90"
3 1/2 yards of main fabric
Total of 3 1/2 yards assorted fabrics
6 yards for backing
2/3 yard for binding

| 9 1/2" | 5 1/2" | 9" | 6" | 9" | 9 3/4" | 5 1/2" | 10 1/4" | 9" | 5 1/4" | 8 1/4" |

| 13" | 6" | 7" | 13" | 7" | 6" | 13" |

Queen
Actual Size of quilt pictured: 88" x 107"
5 1/2 yards of main fabric
Total of 4-5 yards assorted fabrics
9 yards for backing
3/4 yard for binding

| 8 1/2" | 7 1/2" | 8 1/4" | 5 1/2" | 7 1/2" | 10 1/2" | 5 1/2" | 7 1/2" | 10" | 7 1/4" | 7 3/4" |

Finishing

After piecing all the strips together, measure your quilt and trim it where necessary to make it an even width and length.

Piecing together a back for this quilt can be almost as much fun as the front. Use the leftover scraps to piece it together, or find one or two fabrics that you really like and separate them with narrow pieced strips.

Layer the quilt top with batting and the pieced backing, then quilt and bind. Because of the strong vertical lines of the quilt, we chose to quilt overlapping circles of various sizes. Another fun option would be wavy lines running the length of the quilt.

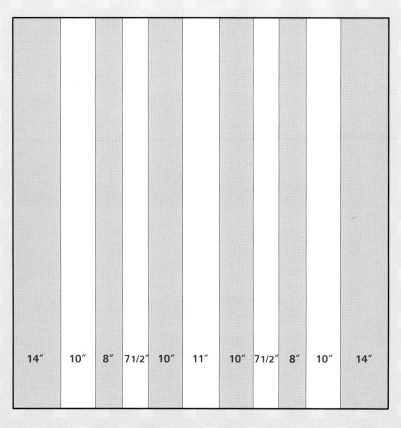

King
Approx. Size: 110" x 110"
7 yards of main fabric
Total of 4-5 yds. assorted fabrics
10 yds. for backing
1 yd. for binding

| 14" | 10" | 8" | 7 1/2" | 10" | 11" | 10" | 7 1/2" | 8" | 10" | 14" |

Whimsical threads

I love the spool block and was messing with several different layouts for various size blocks when mom came up with this one. So simple, yet so effective. We all have scraps of fabrics lying around, so why not use up some of your scraps to make a few spools?

The quilt on page 36 was made from a stash of reproduction fabrics. The one on page 41 is from my collection of Whimsicals fabrics.

Quilt pieced by Jackie Conaway
Quilted by Connie Lancaster

44" x 44"

What's Needed

☐ 1/4 yard each - 8 different browns for spool ends (choose 4 light shades and 4 medium shades)

☐ 1 yard neutral background

☐ Various accent fabrics totaling 3/4 yard

☐ 1 yard dark brown for borders and binding

☐ 3 yards for backing

Cutting the Fabric

We used eight different brown fabrics for the spool ends, four of which were lighter shades of brown so that when the blocks were laid out, we could alternate the light ends with the medium ends.

☐ From the brown spool end fabrics, cut a total of 130 — 1 1/2" x 4 1/2" pieces.

☐ From the background fabric, cut: 32 — 1 1/2" x 6 1/2" strips (A)

Whimsical threads

Cutting the Fabric (cont)

☐ From the various accent fabrics, cut:

16 — 2 1/2" x 6 1/2" strips (D)

16 — 2 1/2" x 4" strips (E)

33 — 2 1/2" x 2 1/2" squares (F)

Make the Spool End Units

Make 130 spool end units as follows: Place a 1 1/2" background square on the end of a brown 1 1/2" x 4 1/2" strip (see Diagram 1.)

Use a rotary ruler and cutter to trim off the corner by lining up the 45 degree line with the edge of the square and the 1/4" line on the diagonal from corner to corner as shown.

Cut off the corner, then stitch your 1/4" seam.

Repeat this on the other end of the brown strip.

NOTE: To reduce bulk in the seams when the blocks are stitched together, press the seams on sixteen of the medium brown units toward the brown piece. Keep these separate, as they will be used on the medium and large spools only. On all remaining units, press the seam toward the light background triangle.

Square these up to 1 1/2" x 4 1/2".

Assemble the Blocks

Stitch a background strip on each side of the corresponding accent piece as shown in Diagrams 2, 3 and 4. Press the seams toward the accent fabric.

Use 8 of the separate medium brown spool end units and 8 of the dark spool end units to complete sixteen large spool blocks. Square these up to 4 1/2" x 8 1/2". (Diagram 2)

Use 8 of the separate medium brown spool end units and 8 of the dark spool end units to complete sixteen medium spool blocks. Square these up to 4 1/2" x 6". (Diagram 3)

Use the remaining spool end units to complete 33 small spool blocks. Square these up to 4 1/2" x 4 1/2". (Diagram 4)

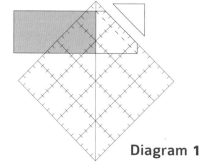

Diagram 1

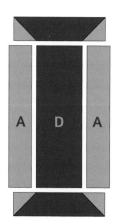

Diagram 2
Square up
to 4 1/2" x 8 1/2"

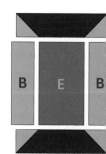

Diagram 3
Square up
to 4 1/2" x 6"

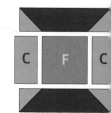

Diagram 4
Square up
to 4 1/2" x 4 1/2"

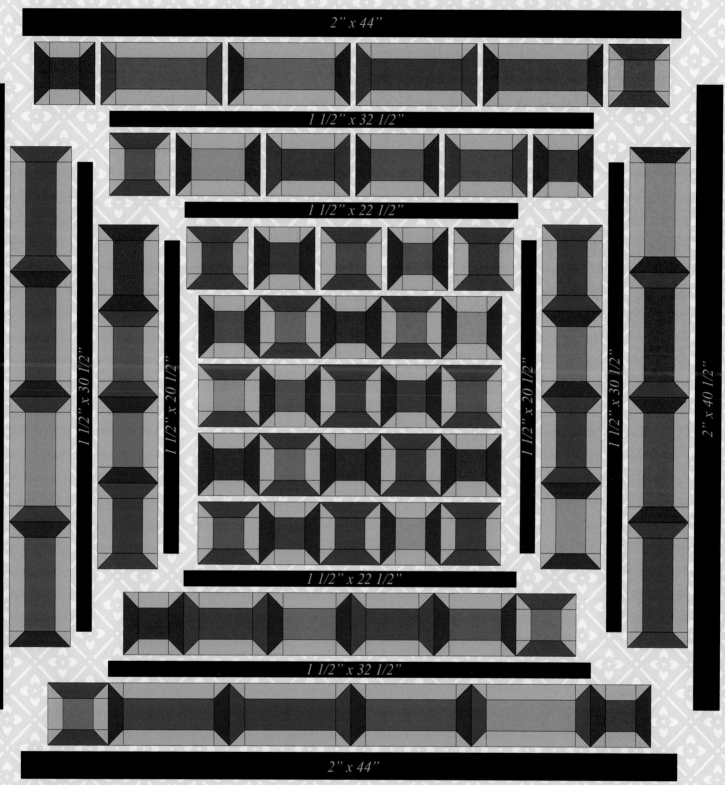

2" x 44"

1 1/2" x 32 1/2"

1 1/2" x 22 1/2"

2" x 40 1/2"

1 1/2" x 30 1/2"

1 1/2" x 20 1/2"

1 1/2" x 20 1/2"

1 1/2" x 30 1/2"

2" x 40 1/2"

1 1/2" x 22 1/2"

1 1/2" x 32 1/2"

2" x 44"

Piecing Diagram

Whimsical threads

Piece the Quilt Together

Referring to the Overall Piecing Diagram, stitch together the center section of small spools.

Make note of your light and medium brown spool ends and alternate between them when piecing together the medium and large spools.

From the border fabric, cut 5 — 1 1/2" strips the width of the fabric. NOTE: If your fabric does not measure at least 44" wide, you will need to cut an extra 1 1/2" strip. Piece these together to make one long strip.

From the border fabric, also cut 4 — 2" strips the width of the fabric. Again, depending on your measurements, you may need to cut one extra.

Suggestion

Before cutting the border strips to length, check the measurements given with your actual measurement and make adjustments as needed.

Add the 1 1/2" inner border, then stitch together the medium spools, adding a small spool on each corner. See photo for direction.

Add the 1 1/2" second border, then stitch together the large spools, again adding the small spools on each corner.

Add the 2" outer border.

Layer this with batting and a backing, quilt and bind.

**Whimsical Threads
by Jackie Conaway
Quilted by Helen
Stingley**

44" x 44"

Crazy strips

I have always been fascinated with scrap quilts. It's fun to look at them and wonder if there was any planning involved, especially when I spot those few mistakes that give it so much character.

However, when I try making a random scrap quilt, I find it hard to put odd colors and fabrics together, throwing caution to the wind, and letting the quilt randomly fall together.

The **Crazy Strips** quilt is our adaptation of an antique quilt that we fell in love with, but wanted to make easier. With ours, we simplified the construction by making twenty large blocks, then cutting them into fourths to make all the smaller blocks. So, although it looks like a lot of pieces, the process was quick and painless. And we ended up with a very random, scrappy quilt! As in the original, you may notice mistakes in some of our squares. But, just as it is with antique quilts, you are left wondering, "Were these planned?" Hmm....you may never know!

Made by
Terri Degenkolb

Quilted by
Marilyn Harding

60" x 75"

What's Needed
- ☐ 20 fat quarters for "crazy" blocks
- ☐ 3/4 yard for inner sashing (A)
- ☐ Fat 1/8 for center squares (B)
- ☐ 1 1/3 yard for sashing/border (C)
- ☐ 1/4 yard for cornerstones (D)
- ☐ 1/2 yard for binding
- ☐ 3 1/2 yards for backing

Crazy strips

Cutting the Pieces

- From the inner sashing fabric (A), cut eighty 1 3/4" x 6 1/4" strips.

- From the center square fabric (B), cut twenty 1 3/4" squares.

- From the sashing/border fabric (C), cut 49 2 1/2" x 13 1/2" strips.

- From the cornerstone fabric (D), cut thirty 2 1/2" squares.

- Make freezer paper templates for block pieces A-J.

Using the twenty fat quarters for the crazy blocks, layer five groups of four fabrics each, all right side up. Position the 10 freezer paper templates on one group of fabrics and iron in place, keeping the outer edges of each template going with the grain line of the fabric. Cut around the templates. Place these close to your machine, laying them out as they will be stitched together (see the Crazy Piece Diagram). Peel the freezer paper templates off and repeat with the remaining groups of fabrics. You need to cut twenty from each template piece.

Assembling the Blocks (Make twenty blocks)

Before beginning to stitch the strips together, "shuffle" the fabrics within each stack to vary their placement in the blocks.

Following the Crazy Piece Diagram, stitch together twenty large "crazy" blocks. Chain piecing works great for this step. Simply take the first A and B pieces off the pile and stitch them together. Without stopping at the end of the piece, take the next A and B off the pile and continue on through the entire stack of twenty! Then, add the remaining pieces in the same manner. Don't stress too much over making the blocks exactly square. We've allowed plenty "oops" room to trim them all down to size!

Trim each "crazy" block to measure 12 1/2" square. Then, cut each one into fourths to make eighty 6 1/4" squares.

Using the inner sashing strips (A) and the center squares (B), piece together twenty blocks as shown in the Block Piecing diagram, turning strip units toward the center of the block to vary fabric and positions. Square these twenty blocks up to measure 13 1/2".

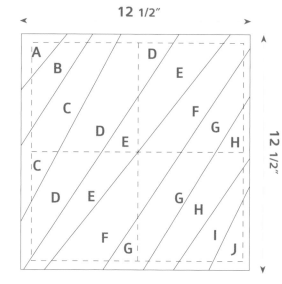

Crazy Piece Diagram

Block Piecing Diagram

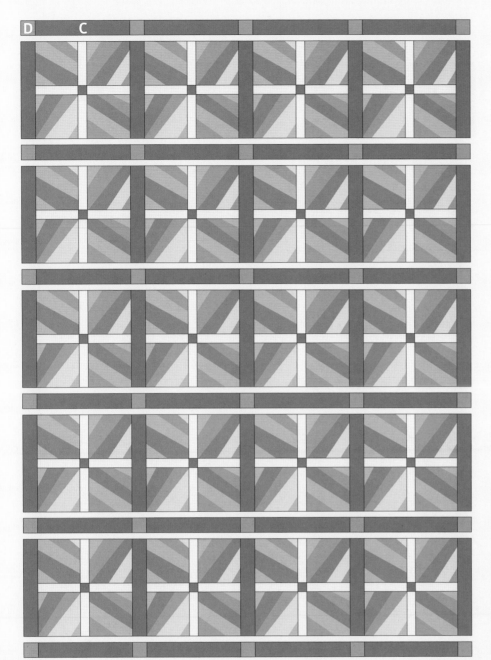

Overall Piecing Diagram

Finishing

Lay out the blocks in five rows of four blocks each, alternating the blocks with the sashing strips (C) and cornerstones (D), ending each row with sashing as shown in the Overall Piecing Diagram.
Stitch together each row, then stitch the rows together, pressing the seams towards the sashing.
Layer with batting and backing, then quilt and bind.

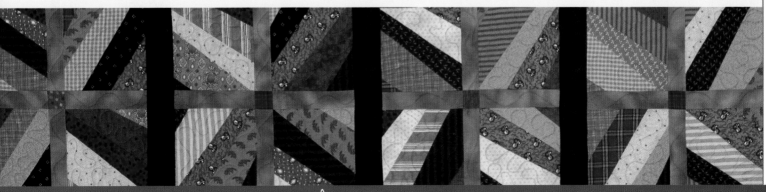

Crazy Strips

Crazy Strips Templates presented in four quadrants – copy and piece together.

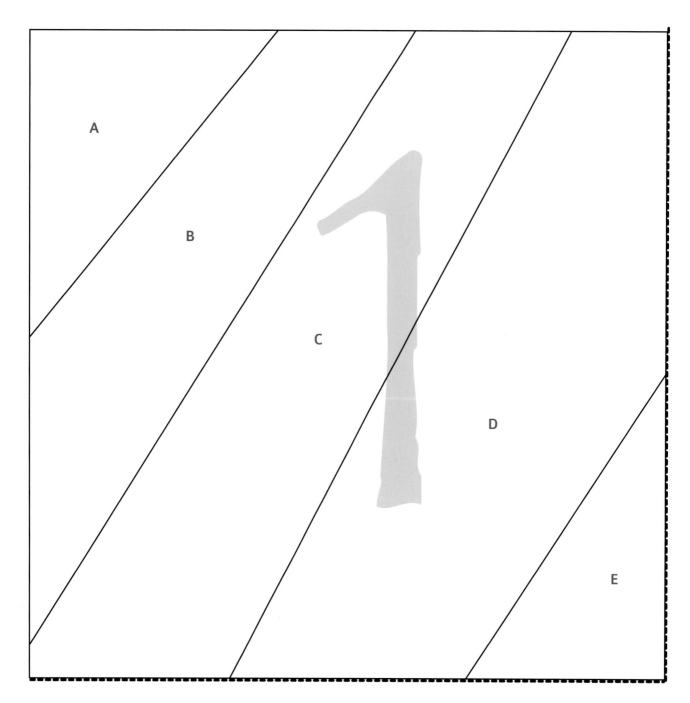

Joins bottom of template on page 48

Joins bottom of template on page 49

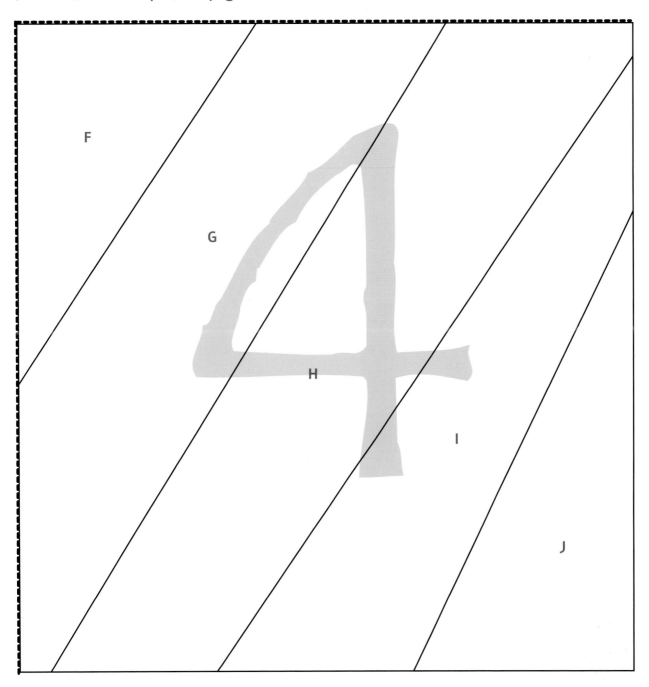

F

G

H

I

J

Not Quite Christmas

These blocks looked so much like poinsettias, we just had to use them in a Christmas quilt. But, not being ones to use those traditional reds and greens, we made it a bit more muted so it could be left out year round, hence the name!

Made by Terri Degenkolb
Quilted by Jackie Conaway

44" x 44"

What's Needed

Flower Block

- ☐ 2/3 yard light brown print for background
- ☐ 1/3 yard brown print for flowers
- ☐ Fat 1/8 gold/rust for sashing
- ☐ Fat 1/8 black print for center
- ☐ Fat 1/8 light green for stem applique

Alternate Block and Border

- ☐ 1 1/4 yard black print for background
- ☐ 1/2 yard gold/rust print for accent
- ☐ 1/3 yard light green for cross sashing
- ☐ 6" x 6" dark brown for center squares
- ☐ 2/3 yard green/gray for sashing
- ☐ 1/4 yard dark brown for cornerstones
- ☐ 3 1/2 yards for backing
- ☐ 1/2 yard for binding

Cutting the Pieces

For the Flower Blocks cut:

☐ Background fabric:

Thirty-two 1 3/4" squares (A)

Sixteen 3" squares (B)

Sixteen 2 3/8" squares (E)

Four 3 3/4" squares for the flying geese (G)

Sixteen 2 3/8" squares for the half squares (H)

☐ Flower fabric:

Sixteen 1 3/4" x 3" strips (F)

Sixteen 2 1/8" squares for the flying geese (G)

Sixteen 2 3/8" squares for the half squares (H)

☐ Sashing fabric: eight 3 3/8" squares (D)

☐ Center fabric: four 41/8" squares (C)

For the Alternate Blocks and Border Cut

☐ Background fabric:

Eight 2 1/4" strips the width of the fabric (A)

Four 1 1/2" strips x the width of the fabric

Four 3 1/2" strips x the width of the fabric for the outer border

☐ Accent fabric:

Three 1 1/2" strips the width of the fabric (B) four 1 1/2" strips x the width of the fabric for the outer border

☐ Cross sashing fabric: twenty 1 1/2" x 7 1/2" strips (C)

Four 1 1/2" x 8" strips and four 1 1/2" x 9" strips for the outer border

☐ Center square fabric:
Five 1 1/2" squares (D)

☐ From the sashing fabric, cut twenty-four 2 1/2" x 10 1/2" strips.

☐ From the cornerstone fabric, cut sixteen 2 1/2" squares and four 5 3/4" squares.

Making the Flower Block: (make 4)

Draw a diagonal line on the wrong side of each background (E) square.

Place the squares on opposite corners of the sashing (D) squares.

Stitch along the drawn lines, press, then trim off the excess.

Cut along the diagonal of each sashing square as shown, to yield sixteen units.

Stitch these corner units to the center (C) square. Square these up to measure 5 1/2".

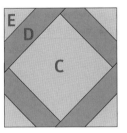
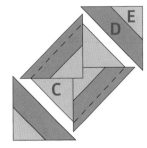

Make sixteen flying geese units with the background fabric (G) and flower fabric (G) as follows:

    Draw a diagonal line on the wrong side of each (G) flower fabric square.

    With right sides together, place two of these squares on opposite corners of the (G) background fabric squares and stitch 1/4" from the drawn lines. (See Step 1) Cut these apart on the drawn line and press. (See Step 2)

    With right sides together, place a flower fabric square on the corner of the resulting unit and stitch 1/4" from the drawn lines. (See Step 3) Cut these apart on the drawn line and press. (See Step 4)

Layer each 2 3/8" background square with a 2 3/8" flower fabric square, right sides together. Cut each pair along the diagonal and stitch the resulting triangles together along the diagonal. Square these up to 1 3/4".

Stitch four flower blocks together as shown in the diagram. Square each one up to measure 10 1/2".

Step 1   Step 2   Step 3   Step 4

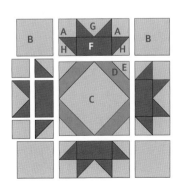

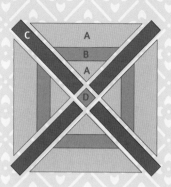

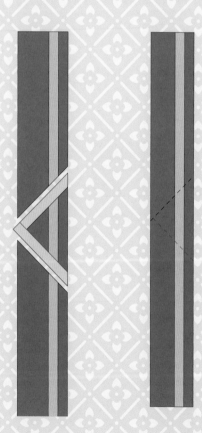

Using your favorite method, applique the stems on each flower block.

Making the Alternate Block (make 5)

Stitch a background strip (A) to both sides of each accent strip(B).

From these pieced strips, cut twenty triangles, as shown in the diagram, using the Triangle Template. The bias edges should measure 7 1/8".

Stitch together five blocks as shown, being careful to not stretch the bias edges on the triangles. Square these blocks up to measure 10 1/2". We found the easiest way to square these up accuarately was to use a 12" square and line the 5 1/4" mark up in the center of the block, trimming all edges.

Adding the Sashing and Border

Referring to the photo, lay out the blocks with the sashing and the cornerstones.

Stitch the quilt center together.

Using the two outer border fabrics, stitch a 1 1/2" strip on one side of each accent strip and a 3 1/2" strip on the other.

Use the Triangle Template to cut one triangle from the CENTER of each of these pieced strips, lining the long edge of the template up with the edge of the pieced borders (see diagram). The remaining strips should measure at least 14" long and will be used on either side of the triangle.

Stitch an 8" sashing strip to a long side of each triangle cut above. On the remaining sides, add the 9" sashing strips. Be careful as you handle, sew and press these, as they are bias edges!

Stitch the triangles to the remaining pieced border units. Cut these pieced borders to 38 1/2" long, centering the pieced triangle.

Stitch a pieced border on two sides of the quilt. Add 5 3/4" cornerstones to the ends of the remaining border strips, then stitch them to the quilt.

Layer with backing and batting, quilt and ENJOY!

Not Quite Christmas

Flower Stem
Prepare 8 for appliqué

Alternate Block
Triangle Template

1

Spring flowers

From the book
Journeys

Made by Terri Degenkolb
17" x 46"

My gardens consist mostly of shade loving plants and weeds. And even though I admire (and secretly want) a garden full of cheerful, colorful flowers, I know it will never happen because I would rather spend my time sewing than pulling weeds and gardening. But, there are many times I long for a vase of freshly cut flowers, so this is my idea for flowers on the table. They are the best kind - they won't dry up or need water, and they always look cheerful!

NOTE - we found that tearing the wool and cotton gave us a worn looking edge that we liked, along with following the true grain of the fabrics. Obviously, this is a personal preference, so if you would rather cut the pieces, by all means, do it!

- Make freezer paper templates of the flowers, vase, and tongues.

- Cut the applique pieces and tongues from the indicated wool using the freezer paper templates. Note that you will need six large tongues from the foundation wool and six large from the backing wool. Cut the flower stems 3/8" wide by the length indicated with each flower template.

What's Needed

- 1/2 yard Aged Muslin or tea-dyed muslin. (Terri used Aged Muslin by Marcus Brothers.)
- Embroidery floss to match wool

Felted wool as follows:

- 1/2 yard for foundation
- 1/2 yard for backing
- 14" x 16" plaid for baskets
- 8" x 12" dark tan for small tongues
- 6" x 7" drak gray for flower 1 centers
- 8" x 8" tan for flower 1
- 6" x 6" gold for flower 2
- 7" x 7" red for flower 3
- 8" x 9" tan plaid for hearts
- 10" x 13" green for stems and leaves
- Basting thread

Cutting the Pieces

- From the muslin, tear a piece 14" x 43".
- From the foundation wool, tear a piece 17" x 46".
- From the backing wool, tear a piece 17" x 46".

Putting it Together

Stitch the six small tongues to the large outer tongues cut from the foundation wool using a blanket stitch and 2 strands of embroidery floss.

Layer these with the remaining large outer tongues cut from the backing wool and stitch together with a blanket stitch.

Position the applique pieces on the muslin foundation and baste in place.

Stitch each piece to the foundation with 2 strands of embroidery floss and your favorite stitches. We like to use a whipstitch on the larger pieces, straight stitches close to the edge on the small pieces and a blanket stitch.

Lay the completed muslin foundation on the wool foundation, centering it. Stitch the muslin foundation to the wool with two strands of embroidery floss and a running stitch 1/4" from the edge.

With the edges of the tongues sandwiched between, layer the backing and the foundations, matching the edges. Stitch around the entire piece with 2 strands of embroidery floss and a running stitch, making sure to catch the tongues in the stitching.

ENJOY!

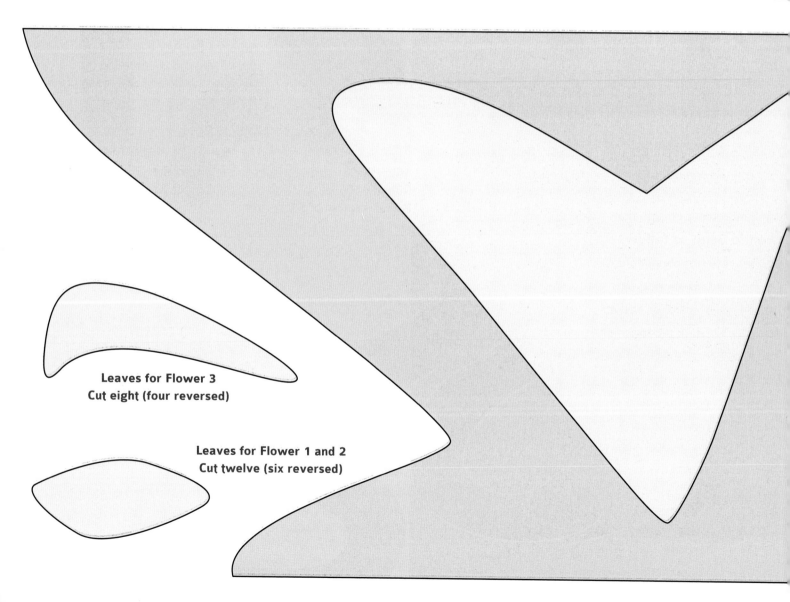

Flower 3
Cut four of each piece
Cut stem 3/8" x 51/2"

Leaves for Flower 3
Cut eight (four reversed)

Leaves for Flower 1 and 2
Cut twelve (six reversed)

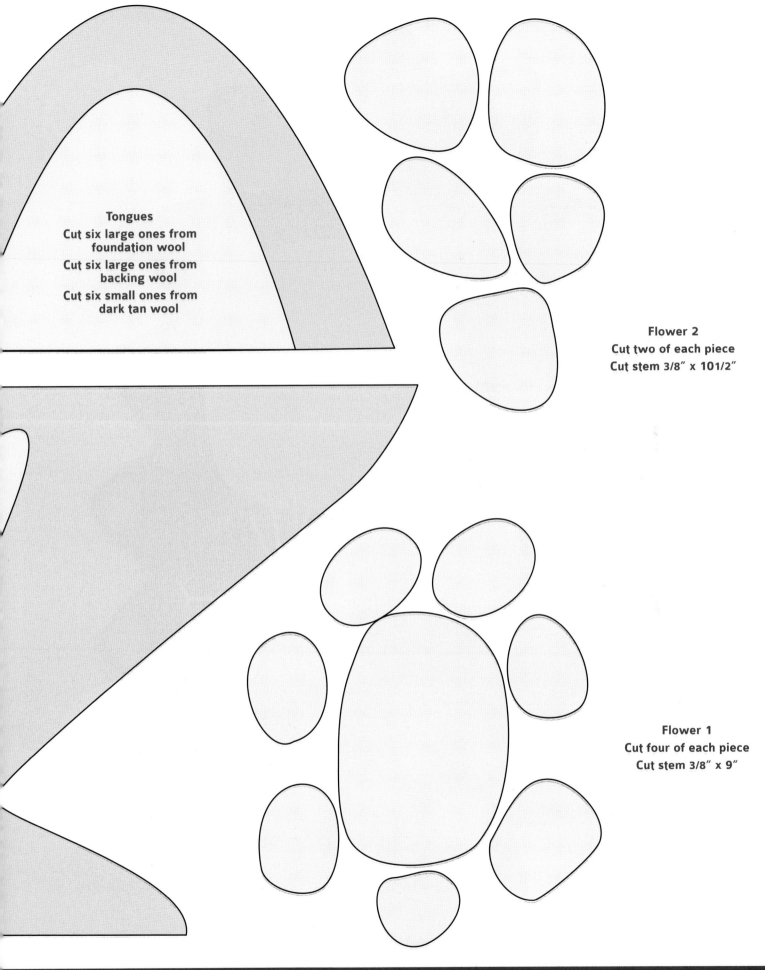

Tongues
Cut six large ones from foundation wool
Cut six large ones from backing wool
Cut six small ones from dark tan wool

Flower 2
Cut two of each piece
Cut stem 3/8" x 101/2"

Flower 1
Cut four of each piece
Cut stem 3/8" x 9"

Pineapple penny rug

They say that the pineapple is a symbol of hospitality and welcome. I don't know if anyone feels more welcome when I have this on my kitchen table, but I hope they do!

Made by Terri Degenkolb

21" x 28"

What's Needed

- ☐ 1/2 yard wool for foundation & tongues
- ☐ 1/2 yard black wool for backing
- ☐ Fat 1/8 gold wool for pennies
- ☐ 12" x 14" gold wool for pineapples
- ☐ 9" x 9" red wool for flowers
- ☐ 10" x 10" green wool for leaves, stems, tops
- ☐ 4" x 4" rust wool for flower berries
- ☐ Embroidery floss to match wool

Cutting the Pieces

Make and use freezer paper templates to cut the pieces from the felted wool. For the foundation template, fold a piece of 18" x 36" freezer paper into fourths. Unfold this and trace the foundation template onto one quarter, placing the dashed lines on the fold lines. Refold the freezer paper and strategically place a few staples to hold the layers together, then cut along the drawn line through all four layers.

From the foundation wool, cut one foundation and sixteen tongues.

From the backing wool, cut one foundation and sixteen tongues.

Cutting the Pieces (cont.)

Cut two pineapples and twelve flower centers from gold wool.

Cut two pineapple tops, two leaves, and two 3/8" x 8 1/2" stems from green wool.

Cut four flowers, reversing two, from red wool.

Cut sixteen pennies from tan wool.

Assembly

Position the pineapples, flowers, stems and leaves on the foundation and baste them in place.

Stitch the pieces to the foundation using two strands of embroidery floss and a whipstitch or blanket stitch. Add the lines to the pineapples by drawing them first with chalk, using the template as a guide, then stitching them on with three strands of embroidery floss and long straight stitches.

Stitch a penny on each foundation tongue. With wrong sides together, layer each foundation tongue with a backing tongue. Stitch around the outside edge of each one with two strands of embroidery floss and a blanket stitch.

Layer the foundation and the backing, wrong sides together. Position the tongues around the edge by sandwiching them between the two layers. Blanket stitch around the edge, through all layers, with two strands of embroidery floss.

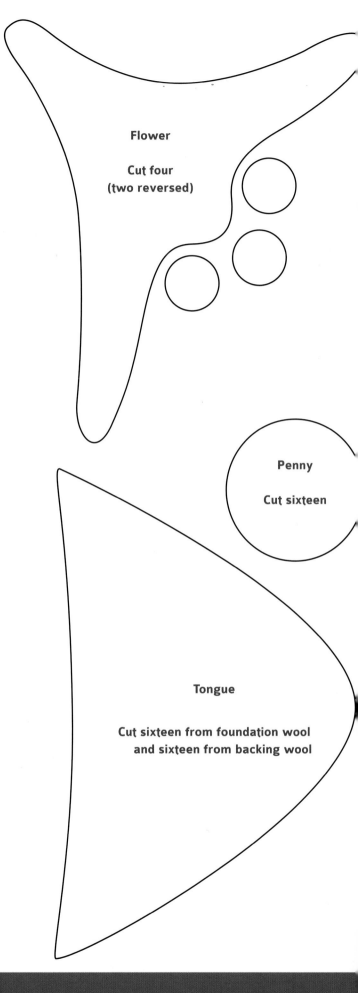

Flower

Cut four
(two reversed)

Penny

Cut sixteen

Tongue

Cut sixteen from foundation wool
and sixteen from backing wool

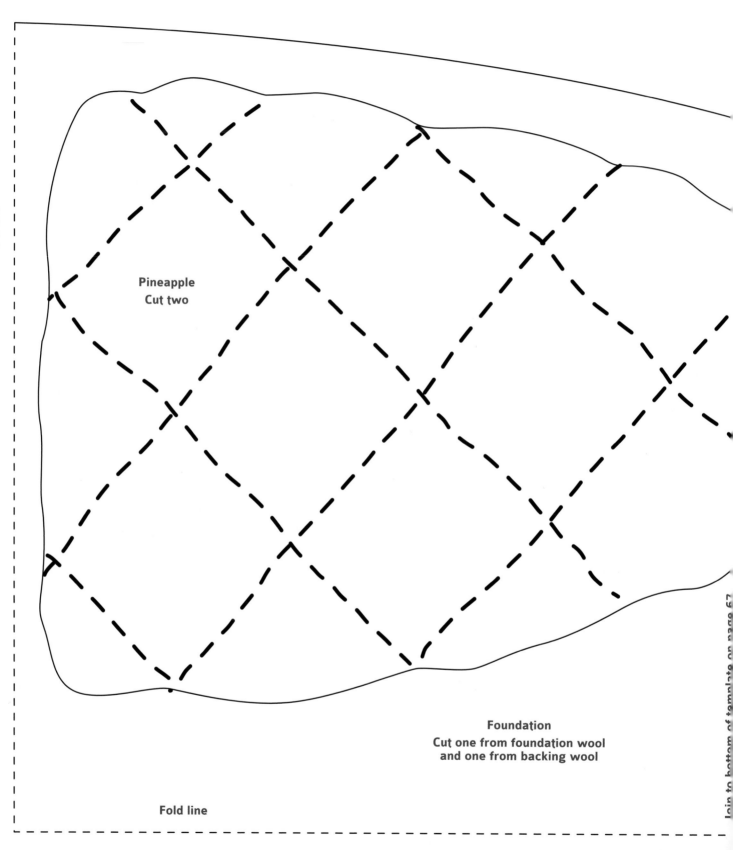

Pineapple
Cut two

Foundation
Cut one from foundation wool
and one from backing wool

Fold line

Join to bottom of template on page 67

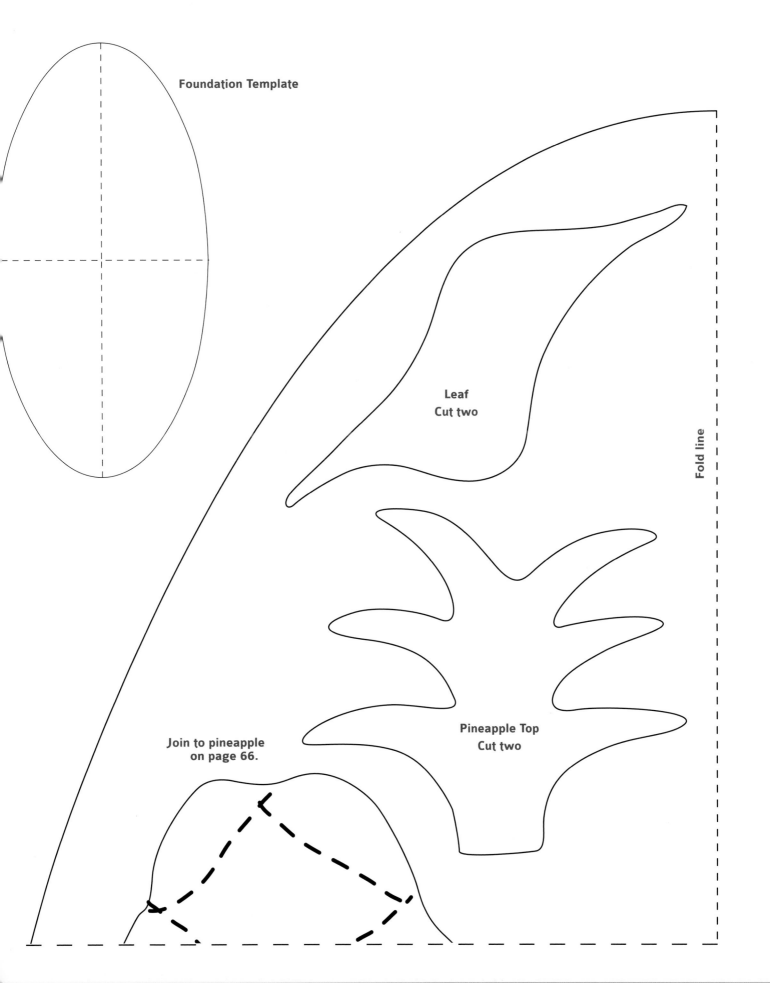

Foundation Template

Leaf
Cut two

Fold line

Pineapple Top
Cut two

Join to pineapple
on page 66.

This pillow is one of my favorites.

Maybe it's the simplicity of it. Or maybe it's because the flowers are made from stars. I love stars. One of my sons has counted the stars hanging or sitting out in our small bathroom and informs me that there are 18 of them. If this pillow would fit, I'd put it in there just to add to the collection.

Made by Terri Degenkolb

16" x 35"

Night blooms pillow

What's Needed

- ☐ 1 yard gray stripe for pillow front and back
- ☐ 13" x 20" gold for tabs
- ☐ 6" x 18" plaid accent fabric for ends
- ☐ 14" square of green for stems and leaves
- ☐ 8" square from each of six prints for flowers
- ☐ 4" square from each of three prints for flower centers
- ☐ Six 1" buttons
- ☐ Stuffing

Cutting the Pieces

- ☐ From the foundation fabric, cut one piece 16 1/2" x 36" for the pillow back and one piece 16 1/2" x 31" for the front.
- ☐ From the accent fabric, cut two strips 3" x 16 1/2".
- ☐ From the tab fabric, cut six 6" squares.

Night blooms pillow

Assembly

To make the tabs, fold each 6" square in half and press. Now, fold each corner down, as shown, matching the raw edges, making a triangle. Press again.

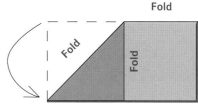

Position three triangle tabs on each of the short ends of the pillow front, matching the raw edges and placing the folded side of the tab against the right side of the foundation.

The triangles should overlap in the seam area, allowing for the 1/4" seam.

With right sides together and the tabs sandwiched between, place the accent fabric strips on the foundation and stitch in place. Press the seams toward the accent strip.

Prepare your applique pieces using your favorite method. You will need three of each flower piece and six leaves. For the stems, cut bias strips 1 1/4" wide, making two strips 10" long and one strip 9" long. To prepare them for applique, fold the strips into thirds, WRONG sides together, and machine baste down the center. When you stitch the bias strip to your foundation, place the side with the raw edge against the foundation.

Position the applique pieces on the foundation and stitch in place. Add a button to each tab.

With the pillow front and back right sides together, stitch around the edges, leaving an opening for turning and stuffing.

After turning the pillow right side out and stuffing it, whipstitch the opening closed.

Cut three of each flower piece

Cut three of each leaf

From the book Journeys

Growing up in rural Indiana we were surrounded by corn fields, and all those little wildflowers along the side of the road were always such a welcome sight to me. I still love to look at them as I drive down the road now, but they are slowly being replaced by ever widening roads and newly manicured flower beds.

When we had cats, I got such a kick out of watching them play in the flowers. Sometimes they would hide in them, like they thought no one knew that they were there, just waiting to pounce on the next person who walked by.

Putting those two memories together in this wall warmer, this little kitty seems to just be relaxing amidst the flowers sprouting around him, and it makes me smile very time I look at it.

Wildflowers

23" x 42"
Made by Terri Degenkolb
Quilted by Jackie Conaway

What's Needed

- 1/2 yard for foundation
- 5/8 yard for main border
- 1/2 yard for accent

Felted wool as follows:

- Fat 1/8 green for letters and leaves
- 7" x 8" gray for cat
- 4" x 4" of four colors for flowers
- Freezer paper for templates
- Embroidery floss to match wool
- 1 1/2 yard for backing
- Fat quarter for binding

Wildflowers

Cutting the Pieces

□ From the foundation fabric, cut the center piece 13" x 32 1/2" (A).

□ From the main border fabric, cut strips:

2 — 1 3/4" x 13" (B)

2 — 2 3/4" x 32 1/2" (C)

2 — 3 1/4" x 13" (F)

2 — 2 1/4" x 32 1/2" (G)

2 — 6" squares for the corner half square blocks

□ From the accent border fabric, cut strips:

2 — 1 1/2" x 13" (D)

2 — 1 1/2" x 32 1/2" (E)

2 — 6" squares for the corner half square blocks

Trace the applique templates onto the dull side of freezer paper. Cut these out and adhere the shiny side of the freezer paper template to the wool with a warm iron. Cut each piece out using the freezer paper as a pattern.

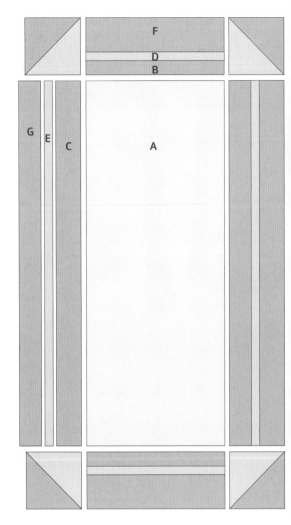

Putting it together

Stitch the border pieces together as shown in the diagram below.

Make 4 half square blocks as follows:

Draw a diagonal line on the wrong side of the two 6" main fabric squares. Layer these with the 6" accent squares, right sides together, and stitch 1/4" on each side of the drawn lines. Cut apart on the lines and press. These are the corner squares. Square these up to measure 5 1/2".

Stitch the borders together as shown, then stitch these to the center foundation piece.

Using the photo as a guide, position the applique pieces on the foundation, then stitch them in place with 2 strands of embroidery floss and a whipstitch. Add the cat's face with 2 strands of embroidery floss and a straight stitch.

Layer with batting and backing, quilt and bind!

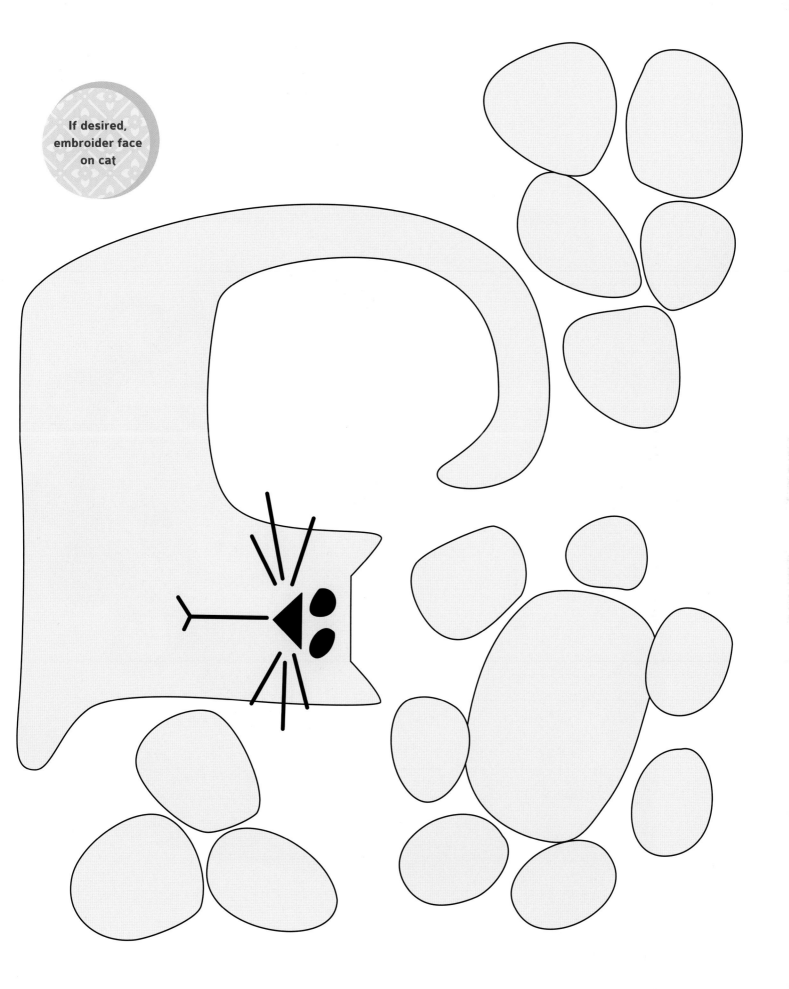

If desired, embroider face on cat

Old Buttons pillow

I've gathered myself quite a collection of old buttons
over the years. I love looking through the antique stores and have even purchased some on ebay. What's great about buttons is that they are small and don't take up much space. I have them in several old jars and even though I will never use all of them, I like the way they look and it's great fun to dump the jar out and search through them for the perfect button.

I originally started this puchneedle project to go on the lid of one of those jars, but I liked it so much, that I had to add some of the old buttons to it. And while I was at it, the rick rack looked great with it too, so one thing led to another....well, you get the picture.

**Made by
Terri Degenkolb**

17" x 17"

What's Needed

- ☐ Felted Wool as follows:
- ☐ 9" square dark gray for punch needle foundation
- ☐ 8" x 8" piece of tan
- ☐ 12" x 15" piece of dark gold
- ☐ Fat quarter of gold/gray plaid for pillow front
- ☐ Fat quarter of gold plaid for pillow back

Old Buttons
pillow

Other supplies Needed

- ☐ Embroidery Floss*
- ☐ Punchneedle and threader
- ☐ Locking embroidery hoop
- ☐ Small sharp scissors
- ☐ 1 yard 3/4" tan rick rack
- ☐ Twelve old buttons
- ☐ 6" square of Form-Flex interfacing
- ☐ Stuffing or a 12" x 16" pillow form

* We used the following:

29 yd. ball of 3 strand floss from Valdani Threads:

color P11 - dark gray

color P12 - chocolate brown

color JP2 - gold

30 yds. of Aged Pewter from The Gentle Art

Trace the reversed design onto the Form-Flex interfacing.
Cut this out as indicated by the dashed line on the template.
(By cutting it to this size, it won't be seen when the foundation
is cut to make the tabs around the design.)

Center this on the foundation wool and fuse it in place.
(The Form Flex makes needle punching on wool much easier
and more secure.)

Place the wool in the locking embroidery hoop.

Punch the design as follows:

Use 3 strands of floss for the entire design.

With the Dark Gray floss, fill in the word and the center
holes of the button.

With the Gold, fill in the top part of the button.

With the Chocolate Brown, fill in the underside
of the button.

Use Aged Pewter to fill in the background.

Punch one row around the background with Gold, add
two rows of Chocolate Brown, then finish with one row of
Dark Gray.

Carefully cut the foundation wool into the shape for the outer tabs, centering the punch needle design. This can be done with a freezer paper template, but be sure to adhere the freezer paper only to the outer part of the wool and NOT onto the punched design to avoid pulling the threads of your design out.

Center the design on the 8" x 8" square of tan wool. Stitch it in place with a stem stitch close to the edge of the design.

From the gold/gray plaid wool, cut a piece 13 1/2" x 17 1/2" for the pillow front. Center the tan square on the pillow front and baste it in place.

From the dark gold wool, cut or tear two pieces 1 1/2" x 13 1/2" and two pieces 3" x 8". Baste these in place around the tan square as shown in the diagram.

Using 3 strands of embroidery floss, stitch all these pieces to the pillow front with a running stitch around the edge of each one.

Add the rick rack to each side, stitching it down with embroidery floss and a running stitch down the center.

Stitch a button to each tab around the punch needle design.

From the gold plaid wool, cut a piece 13 1/2" x 17 1/2" for the pillow back. Stitch the pillow front and back together with a 1/2" seam, leaving an opening for turning and stuffing.

Turn the pillow right side out and stuff, then whip stitch the opening closed.

Basic Punchneedle Supplies

- ☐ Igolochkoy or CTR three strand punchneedle
- ☐ Needle threaders for the punchneedle
- ☐ 8" Locking embroidery hoop (these have lip on them to keep the foundation fabric taut in the hoop)
- ☐ 3 strand Embroidery floss
- ☐ Foundation fabric - I like to use felted wool with Form-Flex interfacing on the back
- ☐ Pair of small sharp scissors

Basic Punchneedle Instructions

Punchneedle is worked from the back of the fabric.

Begin by tracing the design onto the foundation fabric. If you are using the Form-Flex interfacing, trace the design onto the fabric side of the interfacing, then adhere this to the foundation fabric.

Place the foundation fabric in the hoop and tighten the hoop. Working your way around the hoop, pull the foundation fabric very taut making sure that the design is straight.

Thread the punchneedle following the manufacturer's instructions, leaving a 1/2" tail of thread at the tip. When working the design, here are a few things to keep in mind:

Keep the thread coming from the top of your needle loose, without any tension on it.

Hold the needle like a pencil and work with it straight up and down, perpendicular to the fabric.

Keep the needle close to the fabric, dragging it between stitches.

The depth of your stitches will depend on the weight of your fabric. If you are using felted wool, you will need to lengthen your stitches by adjusting the length of the stop on your needle.

When you come to the end of your thread or an area where you need to stop, hold the thread against the fabric and gently pull your needle away, leaving enough room to snip the thread even with the fabric on the back.

Begin by working the small details first, then fill in around them.

Peeking Tom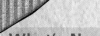

Growing up in the country, we had multiple dogs and too many barn cats to count. I remember when we first moved into our farm house, there was a cat that was left behind by the previous owners. No big deal, except that he must have thought he owned the house because he would randomly show up inside without any of us letting him in. It took us a while to figure out that he was coming in through the crawl space attached to the basement. In all the years we lived there, that was the only cat that was ever allowed in the house.

Since that time, I have had many cats, but right now, I am catless. This little guy is always watching over me in my sewing room and reminds me of all my feline friends I've had over the years.

Made by Terri Degenkolb

10″ tall

What's Needed

- ☐ Fat eighth of gold wool for body
- ☐ 2″ x 2″ of brown wool for nose
- ☐ 1 1/2″ x 1 1/2″ tan wool for outer eye
- ☐ 1″ x 1″ off white wool for inner eye
- ☐ Dark brown embroidery floss
- ☐ Torn strip of homespun 1″ x 20″
- ☐ Stuffing

Preparation

Make freezer paper templates of Peeking Tom's body, his nose and eyes.

Using the templates, cut the pieces from the wool indicated.

Position the nose and eyes on one of the body pieces. Using 2 strands of embroidery floss, stitch them in place with a whip stitch around the edge. For the eyes, first stitch on the larger piece, then add the smaller piece on top. Add 3 large french knots in the center of each eye.

Stitch the mouth, whiskers, claws and ears on with 3 strands of dark embroidery floss and a stem stitch.

Finishing

With right sides together, stitch around the two body pieces with a 1/8″ seam, leaving an opening in the bottom for turning.

NOTE: 1/8″ is enough for felted wool. If wool is not tightly woven, stitch seam twice. A bigger seam will be too bulky.

Carefully clip the curves, then turn the body right side out.

Firmly stuff Peeking Tom, then whipstitch the bottom opening closed.

Tie the torn piece of homespun around his neck.

ENJOY!

Join with feet on page 86